Do You See What I See?

Christmas Coloring Book

Written by
Robin Loisch

Illustrated by
Nikki Boetger

3058002100000175

At Christmas, there's so much to see!

Can you point to a kitten?

Point to the pictures along with me!

Can you point to an angel?

A bright red bird hops all around.

Can you point to a feather?

A bunny watches without a sound.

Can you point to a pine cone?

In our window, candles glow.

Can you point to a bell?

The Christmas wreath has a pretty bow.

Can you point to a candy cane?

Our Christmas tree is shining bright...

Can you point to a cross?

with ornaments and twinkling lights.

Can you point to a star?

My family sets up a nativity.

Can you point to a gift?

I touch the pieces carefully.

Can you point to a flower?

Here is the stable and the hay.

Can you point to a bird?

Mary and Joseph have come to stay.

Can you point to a candle?

Angels, shepherds, and wise men, too...

Can you point to a snowflake?

have come to worship someone new.

Can you point to a lamb?

Baby Jesus, God's only Son, was born on earth for everyone!

For unto you is born this day . . . Christ the Lord.

LUKE 2:11 (KJV)

Can you point to a heart?